MINDFULNESS

Navigate Daily Life Using the New Science of Health and Happiness

BOOK DESCRIPTION

We are what our mind is. This has been an unequivocal conclusion for time immemorial. However, the subject of our mind has never been more relevant. We are experiencing several situations that require mental strength for the survival of the human race. Unfortunately, just like our bodies, our mind is is threatened by complex mind (mental) diseases.

Mindfulness is one of the proven remedies of dealing with the mind disease that is increasingly becoming acute as time goes.

This book, "*Mindfulness: Navigate Daily Life Using the New Science of Health and Happiness*" starts off by introducing you to the subject of mindfulness, its goals, reasons, objectives and importance.

Focusing and concentrating is the core essence of mindfulness. This book unveils key strategies to practicing mindfulness. It also leads you through the entire step-by-step process of practicing mindfulness in ways that you can easily follow and implement.

Many people have become victims of the complexity of modernity. In this complexity, our mind has been bombarded with toxic beliefs that corrupt. Thus, there are many who are suffering from mind diseases. Stress and worry are the leading symptoms of mind disease. Anger and hurt are some of the effects and consequences of this mind disease. This book reveals practical steps on how you can go about healing your mind disease to overcome stress and worry and consequently control your anger and heal yourself.

Compassion is one of the greatest victims of modernity. Unbridled greed characterized by excessive material accumulation, while others hardly meet their need for bare survival are signs of loss of compassion. Lack of compassion is another symptom of mind disease. To be able to regain your compassion and thus promote peace, you have to heal your mind. In this book, the importance of compassion is re-emphasized and how mindfulness can help you regain your compassion is outlined.

Last, but not least, practice makes perfect. Mindfulness is a life-long practice. To remain mindfully fit, you have to cultivate those habits that will enable you to practice mindfulness in each and every moment. This book unveils the Six Habits you need to cultivate in order to succeed in this everyday endeavor.

Enjoy your reading.

GIFT INCLUDED

If you are an entrepreneur, an aspiring entrepreneur, someone who is trying to create additional income stream, or even someone who just loves self improvement books; then you need to read my recommendations for top 10 business books ever. These are book that I have read that have changed my life for the better.

Top 10 Business Books

ABOUT THE AUTHOR

George Pain is an entrepreneur, author and business consultant. He specializes in setting up online businesses from scratch, investment income strategies and global mobility solutions. He has built several businesses from the ground up, and is excited to share his knowledge with readers. Here is a list of his books.

Books of George Pain

DISCLAIMER

CONTENTS

MINDFULNESS 1

BOOK DESCRIPTION 2

GIFT INCLUDED 5

ABOUT THE AUTHOR 6

DISCLAIMER 7

CONTENTS... 8

INTRODUCTION 10

WHAT IS MINDFULNESS? 12

HOW TO REGAIN FOCUS AND CONCENTRATION 24

MANAGING ANGER AND HURT 37

DEALING WITH STRESS AND WORRY 56

PROMOTING COMPASSION AND PEACE 61

SIX HABITS TO CULTIVATE....................................... 71

CONCLUSION 78

INTRODUCTION

There is no greater power than the power of your mind. Yet, many of us look outwardly for solutions to achieve our great aspirations. Lack of satisfaction, peace and happiness are all internal. They are all symptoms of mind disease. Yet, you will not find a hospital in which you will be prescribed a solution for mind disease. Why? Simply because they deal with the diseases of the body, which, to some extent, could just be symptoms of the mind disease.

In this book, you will find not only the mind solution but also the key to that solution. The solution rests well within you. All you need so as to access that key is provided in this book. Yes, you will learn how to regain focus and concentration, manage anger and hurt and, ultimately, be able to deal with stress and worry. All these are the most common symptoms of mind disease. Yet, to have a lasting solution, you inevitably need to promote compassion and peace. Every person who has ever been measured in greatness - prophet, guru, sage, among others, has this one common attribute – compassion.

Practicing mindfulness requires habit. Yet not all habits lead to mindfulness. In this book, you will learn the six habits to cultivate in order to be able to achieve mindfulness in each and every moment.

Keep reading.

WHAT IS MINDFULNESS?

The mind has always been the secret code to untangle humankind's greatest challenges. Great philosophers, prophets, sages and gurus have always alluded to the power of the mind. Their greatness came from their ability to understand this power and utilize it to solve humanity's greatest challenges of their respective times.

The notion of the mind has fascinated many. There are various schools of thoughts in regard to the mind. However, most agree that the mind determines who we become and how we interact with each other and our environment. Mindfulness, being a peculiar mind (mental) attitude, has become an inevitable component of this notion.

So, what is mindfulness?

Mindfulness is a state of self-awareness in an open, caring and conscious way that is free of any judgement.

The Goal of Practicing Mindfulness

The goal of practicing mindfulness is to experiencing life in the moment; to the fullest extent. Experiencing a life in its fullness means;

- Living it fully in the moment without apportioning part of this living neither to the past nor to the future

- Being consciously aware of life as you live it such that no part of it goes to waste (by holding attachments to the past or developing attachments to the future).

- Exposing yourself to fully experience the moment of now without undue reservations.

- Experiencing every moment without attaching your identity to it. When you attach your identity to the moment, it goes into the past with you.

The Key ingredients of Mindfulness

1. Being free to experience the moment of now

2. Being free from judgment

3. Being free from attachment

Being free to the moment of now

Being free to the moment of now simply means that you apply the fullness of your conscious awareness to the moment of now. Being free to experience the moment of now ensures that you not apportion some of your consciousness to what happened yesterday. Similarly, being free to the moment of now allows you not to apportion some of your consciousness to what ought to happen tomorrow. In being free and present in the moment of now, means that you are neither controlled by yesterday nor tomorrow. It is only by being free to experience the moment of now that you can fully be present now. Otherwise, you will partially be present now which is only but a condition of sub-optimality.

Being free from judgment

Being free from judgment simply means you do not attach your opinions to the happenings of now but act as an independent observer to the happenings without disturbing them with your preferences and prejudices. Opinions, preferences and prejudices are based on judgments using criteria from past experiences and hence are already stale and thus cannot be applicable to this moment of freshness. These judgments are like plagues that start attacking the freshness of now and thus turning it into decays of yesterday. A life lived in fullness is a life lived to the freshness of being present in the moment of now.

Being free from attachment

Being free from attachments is the greatest of all freedoms. Being free from attachments doesn't necessarily mean that you are not attached. It simply means that you have power over those attachments such that they do not enslave you. Attachments can cause you pain. They are like anchors to a ship that has already embarked. The result is constant struggle to move on without any motion being experienced but stagnation.

Being free from attachments means that your power to attach and power to detach are fully within your control. When you have power to attach without a countering power to detach, you become a slave to attachments. Examples of situations when you become a slave to attachments are addictions. Another scenario where you lose power to detach is when you still cling to a failed relationship that your consciousness keeps telling you that you ought to detach. In essence, you are addicted to that relationship just as you would be addicted to Cigarettes, Cocaine, Heroin and all sorts of addictive drugs.

The Key Benefits of Mindfulness

Mindfulness has unlimited benefits that cut across all spheres of life. The overall key benefits of mindfulness are;

- Mindfulness heightens your level of awareness

- Mindfulness enables you to be fully present in the moment of now

- Mindfulness enables you to learn to distinguish between you and your thoughts

- Mindfulness enables you to become more connected to your being, the nature of beings and the nature of things.

- Mindfulness enables you to be in harmony with your being, the nature of beings and the nature of things

- Mindfulness enables you to develop self-acceptance which yields self-contentment and self-compassion

- Mindfulness enables you to learn that life is dynamic and thus everything changes. Hence thoughts and feelings come and go.

- Mindfulness enables you to experience calmness and peacefulness

- Mindfulness enables you to experience more balance in your emotions and reactions thus enabling you to be free from the chaos of emotional spikes and outbursts

- Mindfulness enables you to become aware of what you are subconsciously trying to avoid and thus be able to unearth and confront your fears

We will explore these benefits more as we learn about the importance of mindfulness in specific spheres of life in everyday living.

The key reasons why you ought to practice mindfulness

The key reasons as to why you ought to practice mindfulness are immense. Practicing mindfulness enables you to;

- Cultivate contentment

- Build your self-confidence

- Master your own mind

- Live in the moment of now

- Gain the 'power to be me'

Cultivate contentment

Contentment is a condition that exists when you are fully aware of the present. It is an awakening that sees the irrelevance of yesterday and tomorrow to your enjoyment of the present.

Build your self-confidence

Without self-confidence, you live in fear. Fear is derived from past experiences being applied to the present and or extrapolated into the future. Self-confidence is a condition that exists when you feel adequate enough to fully experience the moment of now.

Master your own mind

You need to master your mind. Without mindfulness this would be such a daunting task. Without mindfulness your mind is likely to depose you and become your master.

Live in the moment of now

To live in the moment of now is to relieve yourself off the two unwarranted loads - 'yesterday' and 'tomorrow'. Living in the moment of now makes you light enough to walk in the present as it unveils.

Gain the 'power to be me'

You mind has a map that has been modeled by culture, traditions and past experiences. This map doesn't allow you freedom to experience uncharted path but a predetermined path. Yet, you can never have the 'power to be me' if you are directed by other people via a mind map created through their culture, traditions and teachings. You have to be liberated from your mind maps to experience this.

The key objectives as to why you ought to practice mindfulness

The objectives of practicing mindfulness vary from person to person. However, irrespective of your situation, the following are key objectives;

- To raise one's awareness

- To rise above the control of your mind

- To experience a fulfilling life

- To be happy

Importance of mindfulness

Mindfulness is important to your overall wellbeing. This includes your;

- Physical wellbeing

- Psychological wellbeing

- Emotional wellbeing

The importance of Mindfulness to Your physical wellbeing

Mindfulness allows you to develop conscious awareness of your body. You achieve this by:

- Being consciously aware of your breath

- Being consciously aware of your heartbeat

- Being consciously aware of your posture and form

- Being consciously aware of your diet

How being consciously aware of your breath enhances your physical wellbeing

Being consciously aware of your breath allows you to breath deeper and more regularly. Studies have proven that breathing deeper exercises your chest. In addition, breathing-in deeper allows you to take in more oxygen and as your chest expands to allow greater surface area for the absorption of this oxygen into the bloodstream. Breathing-out deeply removes expired 'air' that is depleted of oxygen and which is also has unwanted germs from the chest.

How being consciously aware of your heartbeat enhances your physical wellbeing

Your breathing helps to regulate your heartbeat. When you are conscious of your heartbeat, you can pace your breathing to help achieve your desired heartbeat. A slow heartbeat is just as dangerous as an extremely high heartbeat. If you are conscious that your heartbeat is too low, you would probably take a faster walk or a run to improve it. In case you realize that it is extremely high, you would put in relaxation measures.

Detecting frequent abnormal heartbeats would also enable you seek medical attention early enough. This can help you reverse onset of heart diseases such as hypertension.

How being consciously aware of your posture and form enhances your physical wellbeing

Being consciously aware of your body enables you to detect even minute discomforts in your posture. Bad posture has been known to contribute to a lot of body aches including back ache, neck ache, joint ache, head ache, numbness of limbs and poor blood circulation (including blood clotting to the extreme limits).

Poor posture cannot allow your mind to be serene and can cause emotional strains. Poor posture leads to bad body form such as unnatural bending of the back. Mindfulness would enable you adjust your body to its natural comfort thus avoiding many physical complications. Mindfulness can also prompt you to do exercises intended to relieve strained body muscles.

How being consciously aware of your diet enhances your physical wellbeing

Studies claim that about 70% of illnesses are caused by poor diet. Being mindful of what you are consuming would enable you be conscious of the consequences of the type of food you are consuming. You would tell that the sugar you are consuming is too high for your body needs, the salt is excessive, there is a lot of fat, the food is stale, and the diet is not balanced, amongst other dietary failures.

Furthermore, having an appropriate diet is just one side of the coin. Digestion and absorption into your body is another crucial side that you cannot ignore. Studies have indicated that eating foods subconsciously could result in indigestion, stomach upsets and mal-absorption. For food to be properly digested and absorbed, your brain has to trigger certain hormones to release the necessary chemicals for digestion and absorption to take place. With your mind being your subconscious, such a trigger cannot be optimized.

The importance of mindfulness to your psychological wellbeing

Psychological wellbeing is achieved when your self-awareness and self-esteem are optimized to such an extent that you can experience freedom and fulfillment. It is by experiencing freedom and fulfillment that you become happy.

The importance of mindfulness to your emotional wellbeing

Your emotional wellbeing depends on both physiological and psychological factors. Lack of physical wellbeing due to lack of exercise has been known to trigger depression. Similarly, lack of self-esteem has been known also to contribute to depression as manifested by self-neglect, self-pity and suicidal tendencies.

HOW TO REGAIN FOCUS AND CONCENTRATION

Mindfulness is about regaining your focus and increasing your concentration to the keep yourself in the moment of now.

Understanding what mindfulness is all about is the first milestone to the way of mindfulness. Understanding why you ought to practice mindfulness becomes the second milestone. Getting to know how to practice mindfulness is the third milestone to the way of mindfulness.

How to practice mindfulness involves three key levels;

- Strategies

- Processes/Procedures

- Exercises

The key strategies to practicing mindfulness

The following are key strategies to practicing mindfulness;

1. Avoid anxiety

2. Focus your attention to now

3. Enhance your power to attach and detach

4. Become nonjudgmental

The key stages in the process of practicing mindfulness

The following statement represents a sequence of events in analogical form that explains the process of practicing mindfulness;

RAIN? STOP! Rest, Meditate

The key stages in the process of practicing mindfulness are;

- RAIN?

- STOP!

- Rest

- Meditate

RAIN

The stage RAIN has several steps that go in tandem with the words that forms the acronym R.A.I.N.

- **R**ecognize

- **A**cknowledge

- **I**nvestigate

- **N**on-align

Recognize

You need recognize the emergence of a strong emotion. By recognizing the presence of a strong emotion in you, then you are in a position to embark on the next stage, acknowledge.

Acknowledge

After recognizing the presence of a strong emotion, you acknowledge its existence. You acknowledge its existence as an energy flow within you. Like an ocean, you recognize this strong emotion as an oncoming wave and like any other oceanic wave, you allow it to pass and go without seeking to confront it or ride on it.

Investigate

Once you acknowledge the existence of this wave of strong emotion, you need to investigate its source. What has caused this strong emotion? Looking at strong emotion as a wave in the ocean, you will realize that every wave in the ocean has its own cause. The cause could be a seismic shock on the ocean bed, a volcanic eruption elsewhere, a strong wind, amongst others. By investigating your emotion, you dig deep into the underlying source so as to unearth it. The key steps involved in the investigation process are;

- **Observe** – Observe without attaching your identity to the occurrence

- **Explore** – Explore the occurrence without disturbing it

- **Learn** – Gather information and derive lessons from your exploration without attaching to it your opinions and identity

- **Understand** – Understand the lessons learned during your exploration

- **Appreciate** – Appreciate that indeed the occurrence was necessary for you to learn

- **Accept** – Accept that events had to occur the way they did without you resorting to the need to apportion blame or being judgmental

- **Respect** – Give due respect to the steps you have taken so far and to yourself for conclusively dealing with them.

Non-Align

To non-align is to be neutral to the occurrences. Just as you watch a wave move in the ocean and become cognizant of its beauty and yet go on with your life after that so would you observe your strong emotion and let it pass on without aligning yourself to it.

STOP

Just like RAIN, STOP is also an acronym that stands for;

- **S**top (what you are doing)

- **T**ake (a breath)

- **O**bserve (your thoughts, feelings and emotions)

- **P**roceed (to that which ought to be done now)

Stop what you are doing

Stop is a powerful word in mindfulness. Being able to stop when you ought to is actually being in charge of your mind. When your mind starts roving into the past, you stop moving with it. The best way to stop moving with your mind is to take a breath. Of course you are breathing. But do take a deep breath in and out with full consciousness.

Take a breath

To take a deep breath is important. It is acknowledging that you have been racing with your mind and you've reached the finishing line and you've got to let it off the mind. Your mind is like the wind and you've no control over it. Let it move on beyond your finish line as you stop to engage in your self-awareness.

Observe your thoughts, feelings and emotions

By observing your thoughts, you are able to act independently of them. Same thing happens with emotions. In observing, you do not identify yourself with your mind but you seek to look at it independently. By this observation, you can gather courage to detach from it and proceed to do something else that is in the present.

Proceed

Proceed to something else that serves you well in the moment. If you get feelings of sadness, move on to call a friend. Chat with your friend. Your friend could be the anti-dote to these negative emotions.

Rest/Relax

Relaxing is the precursor to meditating. It can also take place after meditating.

Meditate

Meditation is the process of bringing yourself back to a state of being by which your self-awareness is optimized. When you meditate, you are able to stop following the maps that have been ingrained into your mind to enable you carry out daily routines.

In meditation you are able to reconnect with your inner being and reflect from within.

Mindfulness exercises to help you regain focus and concentration

The following are important Mindfulness exercises (not in any particular order) to help you regain focus and attention:

Exercise 1: One particular sound from the noise

If you happen to be in a noisy environment, you can choose a particular sound to be mindful about. You could trigger it yourself such as a melody hum from your watch or clock. Alternatively, if there is a certain persistent sound such as that of a bird, frog or hen, or any other persistent sound, be mindful about it. However, the best sound is that from a natural source.

Steps;

1. Sit comfortable and calmly

2. Close your eyes, if necessary

3. Select the particular sound that you want to be mindful about

4. Listen to it

5. Feel its tempo, its timber and resonance

6. Just feel its waves vibrate through you

7. Feel how your body responds and the message it deciphers

While in the process, let thoughts attached to or brought about by noise (unwanted sounds) just pass and go. Recognize them but don't attach any meaning to them.

Exercise 2: Observe your heartbeat

1. Sit in a comfortable serene position.

2. Relax your body muscles, and more so, your chest muscles.

3. Feel your heartbeat.

4. Focus on the heartbeat. Start counting the beats for a while maybe up to 60 heartbeats just to help your mind focus inwards to the heart.

5. Once the mind is focused on the heartbeat, stop counting and just continue feeling the heart beats.

Let thoughts raze, come and go. Do not attach any significance to them. Just recognize that they are thoughts and let them go.

Exercise 3: Focus your mind on the taste of the food that you eat

1. Get a delicious meal.

2. Sit comfortably and relax for a moment.

3. Take food in small bits into the mouth.

4. Chew as you maximize your attention to how it tastes.

5. Feel the different tastes within the bit of food that you are chewing.

6. Swallow it after chewing enough,

7. Make sure that food completely empties in the mouth before taking in another bit of food.

8. Repeat steps (3) to (7) until you have had enough.

While eating, keep off music, TV, conversations and other distractions. The focus should be on the meal. Realize the importance of food to your nature of being. Discover how this holy activity is the second most sacred of all activities (of course, second to pneuma – breathing). Just give up your thoughts to it during your moment of eating. Nothing is more sacred than the air you breathe and the food you are eating. Nothing!

Exercise 4: Observe your breathing

1. Sit in a comfortable serene position.

2. Observe your inhalations and exhalations.

3. Feel the air flow in through your air pathways.

4. Feel it hit your nasal walls and pharynx.

5. Feel the air flow to your deepest part of inhalation.

6. Feel the air go out.

7. Feel it reach the faintest moment of its exit.

While observing your breathing thoughts may come and go. Don't attach much attention to the thought. Let the thought go as it came. Like a clear, odorless, formless, boundless air, let your mind be.

Exercise 5: focusing your mind on a particular aroma/scent

Get a healthy organic scent that you recognize. You can use a scent from one of the essential oils;

Steps:

1. Sit in a comfortable and relaxed position

2. Open up a bottle of scent and place it in front of you

3. Close your eyes

4. Once you sense the scent, make a slow deep inhalation

5. Let it flow within your environment

6. Feel it enter your nostrils and spread through your nerves to the brain and heart

7. Feel it seize the rest of your body

8. Feel its relaxative magic on your muscles

Exercise 6: Switch to your inner eyesight

You may opt to close the eyes.

Steps;

1. Using your inner eyesight, see the crown of your head

2. Scan through your skull as if your inner eyes are a kind of a light torch

3. Scan the brain and move down through the nostrils and via the mouth to the throat.

4. Spread your scan from one shoulder via its arm right through its fingers into the fingers of the next hand backwards to the shoulder and back to the chest.

5. Scan inwards to the heart

6. Move downwards to the liver and then reach the stomach

7. Scan the kidneys

8. Scan the pelvic bone

9. Go down scanning taking one lower limb through the thigh downwards to the leg via the knee and proceed to the foot via the ankle.

10. Exit via the toes and enter the next lower limb via its tows and repeat the same as you did with the first lower limb but in reverse direction till you reach back to the pelvis

11. Climb your scan from the pelvis to the spinal cord

12. From the spinal cord follow the vertebrae to the skull through the bones and back to the eyes.

In this process, recognize thoughts flowing if they do come and just let them be – simply thoughts. Detach from them.

Exercise 7: feel the touch of your beloved pet (it can also be your loved one)

1. Hold your beloved pet.

2. If it's a cat or dog, as you would hold a baby that wants to sleep.

3. Feel its fur, feel its warmth.

4. Feel its breath.

5. Feel its heartbeat and blood flow vibrations.

6. Watch it surrender to you in peace and serenity. Feel the same running within you.

7. Feel your souls synchronized in this peace, calmness and serenity.

Let go off all thoughts. Let them pass as they come. Just be mindful of the peace, calmness and serenity that you are currently experiencing. Appreciate that relationships can at times be healed by simply being calm, peaceful and detaching yourself from thoughts about it.

MANAGING ANGER AND HURT

Anger and hurt (not physical hurt) are the two common symptoms of emotional challenges. They are the consequences of our negative emotions. Some of the negative emotions may be justified while others are not. Yet, allowing them to uncontrollably or overwhelmingly consume our being is not healthy.

The following are key steps we can take in order to manage our anger and hurt;

1. Make a bold decision

2. Take control of your situation

3. Take charge of your emotions

4. Be focused

5. Engage the right association

6. Give meaning to your life

Make a bold decision

Life is about choices. Every moment there is a choice to make – to wake up or not, to breath or not, to eat or not, to go to work or not, to go to school or not, among so many others. Forget about the common misstatement "I have no choice"! There is no situation where you have no choice. Every situation has a choice. Maybe the options may not be such appealing or desired, but, there is a choice nonetheless. Without choices there is no life. Yet, every choice has a consequence.

There are certain key ingredients that characterize a choice;

- Intent
- Timeframe
- Effort

Intent

There is no choice without an intent/purpose. What is your intent in making a certain choice? That determines the value that you have decided to assign your choice. For example, you can choose to snap out of endlessly mourning over your loved one or you can choose to steep yourself into the depth of mourning, continuing to dig more and more every passing day till your life ceases to be. Conversely, you can choose to decide that bygones are bygones. You have no control over what happened. You cannot change the past and hence decide to snap out, recollect yourself and be ready to confront the future and you become self-aware of the present that the moment of now has gifted you. Thus, your intent determines the extent to which your life hurts.

Timeframe

Every choice must be made within a certain timeframe, not just time. Time is limitless. It is only a 'frame' of it that you have cut out that is limited. For a decision to be termed as a decision, it must have a time frame within which it has to be implemented. For example, when do you decide to get over with divorce? To get over with the death of a loved one? You can choose to procrastinate as you wait for the event to miraculously happen by itself or you can make a bold decision to get over it right now, in this very present moment! Life continues to hurt the moment you surrender your bad situation to procrastination.

Effort

Effort is energy in action driven towards achievement of a certain specific intent. Energy that is not driven towards a certain specific intent is not effort but wasted energy. Whenever there is effort, it is always driven towards countering force – inertia. It is only after there is enough force to overcome inertia that things starts moving from potential to kinetic (energy in action). Yes, your world starts moving the moment you overcome your inertia (procrastination, dwelling in the past, exploring your pain, etc). The same applies to hurting. Life hurts for so long as you don't put effort in to push it away from a hurting situation.

So, what is a bold decision?

A bold decision is a one where the various elements of its choice are fully optimized. Yes, it is optimized when the intent is the most supreme of them all (with the highest possible opportunity cost); the timeframe is of utmost priority and the effort is fully dedicated.

Take control of your situation

There are things within our control and there are things that we have no control over such as the weather. People with mental health issues will often spend much time and energy on things that they have no control over. Be mindful of the amount of time you are spending thinking about things that you cannot change or are unhelpful to you. For example, if you are feeling angry or sad about things that have happened to you in the past this is not something that you can change. The past is in the past and you cannot change this. Energy spent dwelling on this past is wasted energy.

Many times, we spend a bigger part of our lives trying to move huge mountains when probably what we require was simply to acknowledge and admire their uniqueness. We only needed to make a step to climb them, see what is hidden beyond them and appreciate the panoramic view of that newness that we soon needed to discover.

You are the world without which it cannot exist. Change yourself and you will indeed change the world. It all begins with your mindset. The greatest determinant of what you can change and what you cannot change is your willpower. This willpower is fuelled by a very powerful propellant – your ATTITUDE. Your attitude determines your willpower. Yet, your attitude and willpower are both products of your very own mindset.

What are the things that you cannot change?

You cannot change;

- **Your past** – Your past happened and it cannot be changed. What matters are the lessons you learned. Don't attach yourself to past occurrences but derive pure lessons for future applications.

- **Your future** – Your future is not yet born. You are not certain that you will live it. Thus, it is good to plan for it, but, don't let it sweep away your joys of the moment. Don't let it take away more than a fair share of what it deserves.

- **People's perception of you** – For so long as you are not alone, there will always be people's perception of you. There is nothing you can do to change people's perceptions but there is everything you can do to change yourself.

What are the things that you can change?

- **Your attitude** – Your attitude drives you. It is the ignition key to your willpower.

- **Your willpower** – Your willpower is the kinetic energy that propels you to take appropriate action to change. Make sure that you are full of it.

- **Your self-image** – Your self-image is a reflection of who you think you are. Sometimes your self-image can be true or false. You need a true self-image in order to discover your true being, purpose and aspirations.

Take charge of your emotions

Other than physical hurt, emotional hurt is one of the most commonly talked about pains in life. In fact, more people encounter emotional pain than physical pain. The most enduring elements of a hurting life are rarely physical but emotional.

It is quite obvious that everyone has experienced emotions in one way or another at varying degree. Just like love, emotion is one of those areas that, although their experience is easy to tell, there is no exact universally agreed definition.

To be able to take charge of your emotions, the most fundamental step is to understand what they are, what their purpose is, how they come about and how you can intelligently apply them to fit different situations.

What is Emotion?

Emotion is a psychological state characterized by interaction of the following key components; subject experience, psychological action and behavioral action.

Subjective experience (how we experience the emotion): Experiencing emotions is highly subjective and depends on one's background, culture or environment. However, the following are common subjective labels; 'angry', 'sad', 'annoyed', 'joyful', 'happy', etc. These are relatively universal though their intensity varies from person to person.

Physiological response (how our body reacts to the emotion): Heart palpation from fear and stomach lurches from anxiety, are some of the physiological reactions. Sweating palms, heart beats and rapid breathing are some of the common physical responses that occur during an emotional encounter.

Behavioral response (how we behave in response to the emotion): This is the action part – the actual expression of emotion. Common expressions include smile to indicate pleasure, happiness, joy or satisfaction; a frown to indicate displeasure or sadness. Emotional intelligence enables one to appropriately interpret these behavioral responses.

How do emotions come about?

Emotions are created or triggered in the brain. Thus, they are a function of the brain. Hence, that which affects or influences the brain has the ability to affect or influence our emotions. This is very important as it helps us understand that we can develop and enhance our emotional intelligence by working on our brain neuro-circuitry – and, of course our mindset.

Emotional intelligence

Emotional intelligence refers to the capability of human beings to recognize their own and other people's emotions, to differentiate between different feelings and tag them appropriately, to apply emotions in guiding thinking and behavior, and to manage or alter them so as to achieve one's goals or adapt them to an existing environment.

According to Daniel Goleman, an expert in emotional intelligence, there are five core competencies of emotional intelligence:

- **Self-awareness** – This is the ability to know oneself including one's emotions, weaknesses, strengths, goals, core values, drive, recognizing their impact on others and making appropriate decisions to achieve their desired intent.

- **Self-regulation** – This is being in control of one's disruptive emotions and impulses and redirecting them to adapt to changing circumstances.

- **Social skill** – This is a skill set that enables one to manage relationships and lead people to a desired direction in order to achieve a desired outcome.

- **Empathy** – This is the ability to put into consideration other people's feelings and factoring them as part of decision-making process.

- **Motivation** – This is the ability to drive oneself towards achievement of certain objectives.

How to boost one's emotional intelligence

The five key competencies inform us of the key areas that we have to improve on in order to boost our emotional intelligence. Ensuring that each of these key competencies is optimized is the best way to boost one's emotional intelligence.

The following are some of the ways to boost each of these core competencies;

- **Boosting self-awareness**: You can boost self-awareness through mindfulness meditation.

- **Enhancing self-regulation**: Self-regulation is about the power to take charge of your emotions. This so much to do with your willpower, so, you have to increase your willpower.

- **Building stronger social skills**: Stronger social skills can be built by engaging the right association through social activities and team-building efforts.

- **Deepening empathy**: The best way to deepen one's empathy is by practicing compassion; both self-compassion and compassion towards others.

- **Increasing one's motivation**: Motivation can be enhanced by challenging yourself to make bold decisions, taking control of your situation and being focused.

The importance of emotional intelligence and willpower in healing a hurting life.

Both emotional intelligence and willpower are a function of the mind. We've seen how the most enduring element of a hurting life is emotions. A lot of times, we are emotionally hurt not because of the deliberate intents of our loved ones but from our misinterpretation and misunderstanding of their emotional expressions and behaviours. Indeed, the biggest and most significant portion of or emotional pains are due to our very own misinterpretations and misunderstandings. Emotional intelligence helps us avoid these misinterpretations and misunderstandings thus significantly cutting down on the sources of our emotional pains. With emotional intelligence we can decrease the incidences and mitigate the damages to our emotions.

With willpower, we can be able to make bold informed decisions with regard to what we have gathered through our emotional intelligence. It could be a bold decision to walk out of a relationship that no longer serves your highest aspirations. It could be a bold decision to accept that your loved one has moved on and it is no longer tenable to keep following him/her expecting them to change their minds thus getting more hurt in the process.

Yes, with a great emotional intelligences accompanied by strong willpower, you can easily take charge of your emotions and go a long way in healing a hurting life.

Be Focused

Focus is a mental phenomenon. When you are mentally disturbed, such as when you are filled with worries, anxiety, stress and even depression, there are plenty of thoughts razing through your mind such that you cannot focus on a certain specific thought that is of importance to your present needs.

Thus, the best way to be focused is to de-clutter your mind from these razing thoughts. A mind that is free is a focused mind. Yet, for this mind to be free, it must not be tethered to the past nor catapulted to the future. It must be free to the present unwrapping in the moment of now.

Engage the right association

We humans are social beings. Without social interactions, the worth of a human being declines to zero. This is why most lonely people raze with suicide thoughts in their minds while some actual commit to these thoughts. Without others, you cannot be. Thus, to be a better you, to become all you need to be, you must engage the right associations. The greatness of a person is the association that he keeps. This is evidently true in business, in profession, in politics, and in all faculties of life.

Thus, to engage the right association is to experience life joys. To engage the wrong association is to experience life hurts. The choice is yours! Make yourself happy.

There is that kind of natural repulsion that happens when you try to engage friendship with a person who isn't interested. Becoming someone's friend is such a subtle natural selection that depends so much on your inner being. It depends so much more on your emotional intelligence than anything else. It is more of a gut feeling. When you try to force a friendship that doesn't or ought not to exist, life will inevitably suck. When you allow yourself to experience the spontaneity of friendship as it arises, you will experience a happy, joyful life.

Yet, friends are not just for interaction. Friends shape you and in the process you shape them. You become one in so many aspects. That's why it is easy to know and understand someone by studying the company that he/she keeps. Hence, if you want to be judged well, then, keep the right associations! To become a better you, a joyful you, a happy you, keep the right company and surely life won't hurt.

Your associations become your lifestyle. Without associations, there is no lifestyle! Thus, if there is a certain kind of lifestyle that you admire or aspire to have, seek association with people who are already living it. Work towards it. This is the ultimate wealth that you can ever acquire. All other forms of wealth will ultimately fall in line.

You cannot forge your associations just as you cannot forge your friendship. This can only come from your inner desire. This must be cultivated by the efforts of your emotional intelligence. Your associations are like the climbing stairs. Having stairs does not guarantee you to the top; they only provide the ways and means. It is up to you to take the action of climbing on the stairs to the top. It is up to you to marshal your sinews to continue climbing, resting if you must, but not giving up midway. It all depends on your will and power – the willpower.

Your relationships are a great investment - probably the richest investment that you could ever have. Like any other shrewd investor, you don't want to keep dead investments. Investments that consume more than they bring are not worth keeping. Keep reviewing your relationships, and those like branches that no longer bear fruits, prune them off so that those that bear fruits can have healthier ones.

Negative people are like very low ceiling that prevent you from standing up, leave alone jumping. They affect your self-esteem, self-confidence, self-worth and self-actualization. They are a disaster to your wellbeing. The earlier you keep them off the better you are back on track to optimizing your potential to becoming all you've ever dreamt of becoming.

Life hurts when you are constrained. Frustrations are simply energy of a potential that has not been allowed to actualize.

If you really want to change the way you have been, then, seek change-makers in your relationships. Yes, people who show you a different perspective of life; People who see opportunities in what you can only see as problems; people who are ready to take your hand and help you make a giant leap over an obstacle; people who are ready and willing to go an extra mile just to make sure that you don't give on your resolve. These are the change-makers that you need! Life will stop hurting when you embrace such people.

Tips to help you engender the right association;

- Know **what** you want out of this association

- Know **why** you need what you want in this association

- Know **where** to get the people with what you need

- Determine **when** to meet the people with what you need

- Establish **how** to get the people with what you need

Give meaning to your life

Life is so simple, life is so basic. Yet, many of us waste it chasing glitters beyond the horizon. Do we have time just to walk barefoot on grass and just feel its effect beneath our feet? Do we have time just to watch the marvels of a waterfall and just be without thoughts ringing about our job, business, yesterday and tomorrow? The greatest of miracles happen not in great things but in the small things that we overlook. Just watch safari ants matching and building their path, guarding and ferrying foodstuff to their new kingdom. As blind as they are, they probably work more miracles than that which we achieve in bellowing factories.

The real meaning of life is not in the big things but in the small things that we so often take for granted. Life hurts when we take for granted small things like just sitting calm and taking a deep breath; playing around just to have fun; tending to a small garden – be it in your backyard or in your in-house pot; spending time to fetch clean, natural, organic ingredients for the meal that you are going to cook; playing with your lovely pet; having time to play with children; visiting and spending time with your parents/grandparents, etc. It is such small activities that absorb the shocks of the hurts of life leaving you to ride comfortably to your life's destiny.

Have you ever postponed that nice stanza of poetry that just ran in mind simply to be some place on time? Have you ever muted that sound of music that had started reverberating in your vocals simply because it wasn't the 'right' time? Well, those were the moments of true living that you wished away as you were getting ready to live them later, only for the 'right' time to come and you realize that the poem and the lyric are gone to the world of the forgotten never to come back. That's a piece of life died with the poem and the music, forever!

Opportunities such as these are plenty and come spontaneously. They knock quite often. It all about how prepared you are to grab them and drink from the sweet potion they present. Life hurts when you miss to partake from such opportunities simply because you weren't prepared. Carry with you a pen and a notebook. Carry with you a camera. Carry with you a voice recorder. These are the little things that you can carry around without feeling weighty yet can grab great moments. Yes, life hurts when you let opportunities fizzle away from you. Seize the moment!

Just as we keep away our poems and music, is the very same we keep away our eternal life. A life not fully lived in its very moment is a life that has lost its eternity. A poem lost is a poem untold. A song lost is a song unsung. How else would we impact others if not through that poem and music? How would our loved ones been if they had listened to our poem and danced to our music? What a lasting inspiration would you have bequeathed your loved ones had they listened to your poem and danced to your music?

An eternal life is that life that continues to impact your loved ones and others for years and years long after you are gone. An eternal life doesn't depend on how long you live, but on how much you transformed yourself to positively impact with a lasting legacy generation after generation.

An eternal life is a one lived fully in the moment of now. It is a one that bequeaths others with a legacy free from hurts and salvages them from their very own hurts.

The fact that your coming into birth was an effort of many people and your very upbringing an effort of even a bigger multitude, it simply means you owe your life not just to you but many others - gone, living and yet to come. Live your life so that others may easily live. Leave a path so that others may have their journeys easier because you lived to create it. This is the essence of eternity.

DEALING WITH STRESS AND WORRY

By far, the greatest goal of practicing mindfulness is to attain mental and psychological wellbeing. Yet, stress and worry are characteristic of lack of mental and psychological wellbeing.

Meditation is the most powerful too you can employ to your mindfulness to deal with stress and worries.

Mindfulness meditation is great for your;

- Mental wellbeing

- Psychological wellbeing

Mindfulness meditation for your mental wellbeing

Mindfulness for your mental wellbeing is aimed at:

- Boosting your attention

- Increasing your brain power

Mindfulness meditation clears your mind of unnecessary distractions

Your mind is a random pulse generator. Every pulse is a thought that comes out and requires attention. You cannot stop this pulse generator. However, through meditation, you can focus your attention away from its razing thoughts. This allows your mind power to deal with that which is within your control - the happenings of now.

Mindfulness meditation to increase brain power

Physicists always say that power is energy in action. Brain power is no exception. To increase power, just as in light rays or electric current, it needs to be concentrated and focused towards a certain given direction. This works the same way with your brain power.

Mindfulness meditation helps to increase brain power by concentrating and focusing your mental energy towards a particular end – be it experiencing your inner being, studying, working or otherwise. This brain power, when practiced for a long time, grows and lasts longer, much beyond the meditation time. Thus, this brain power becomes available to be utilized for other functions.

Mindfulness meditation for your psychological wellbeing

Mindfulness meditation is largely a psychological endeavor which as an effect on other faculties of your wellbeing.

Mindfulness meditation for your psychological wellbeing is aimed at;

- Resetting your mindset

- Engendering positive attitude

- Overcoming bad habits

- Reducing stress

Mindfulness to reset your mindset

A mindset is a set of beliefs, assumptions and thoughts that make up one's mental attitude, habits, inclination or disposition which predetermines a person's perceptions and responses to situations, circumstances and events.

More often than not, our mind is set up in such a way that our thought process goes along certain predefined patterns, commonly referred to as mental maps. These mental maps are created by the process of tradition, schooling and experiences which all belong to the past and have very little or no bearing at all in the moment of now.

Thus, to truthfully experience the present, that is, the moment of now, you have to reset your mindset. Resetting your mindset is in essence deleting or rather erasing these thought patterns which brings about judgments based on standards of the past.

Why is mindset so important?

Mindset is such important because it is the point of reference to which you perceive and respond to events, circumstances and situation. How you perceive things depends on your mindset. That's why many experts say that 'you see things as you are' and not necessarily as they are. This 'you are' is your mindset.

Mindset is the fertile ground upon which the seed of vision grows. How healthy and great your vision becomes solely depend on your mindset. A defective mindset will definitely yield a defective vision. A fixed mindset will yield a fixed vision. And thus, a transformational (growth) mindset will yield a transformational vision.

Mindfulness to engender positive attitude

It is commonly said that your attitude drives you. This is true. Your attitude determines your perspective in life, what to do and how to do it. It also determines your experiences. This is because your experience is really not that which happened to you but how you responded to it. This response, unless reflex, highly depends on your past – your tradition, your lessons and experiences of similar situation either as happened to you or others whom you got to witness as to how they responded.

Mindfulness to overcome bad habits

A habit is a recurrent, (mostly unconscious), pattern of behavior that is achieved through frequent repetition.

Mindfulness to reduce stress

The greatest contributor to stress is our mindset, attitude and habits. Regrets about the past and worries about the future are some of the things that bring about stress. Mindfulness meditation, while helping you to focus on the present, diverts your attention away from your past and future thus avoiding these two key triggers of stress.

PROMOTING COMPASSION AND PEACE

Compassion can simply be stated as passionate love for humanity. Compassion is a feeling that arises when you are confronted with the suffering of another that pushes you to have an inner compulsion, force or desire to relieve that suffering.

Studies have indicated that compassion is a necessity for the survival of the human species.

The benefits of compassion are many and immense. The following are just but a few of them;

- Compassion makes us feel good. Studies have found out that a compassionate deed triggers the 'feel good' part of our brain circuitry responsible for pleasure and reward thus leading happiness.

- Being compassionate boosts the positive effects of the Vagus nerve thus helping to slow down the heart rate which, in the long-run serves to reduce the risk of heart disease.

- Compassion lowers the stress hormones in the blood system and saliva, thus boosting the immune system and helping people become more resilient to stress.

- Compassion reduces worries about the past and anxiety about the future thus helping to prevent risks of mental disorder.

- Compassion triggers neurons in the brain which are responsible for parental nurturance thus helping to develop and boosts one's care-giving attributes which are important in personal development and leadership.

- Compassion boosts relationships by engendering optimism and supportive communication between partners.

- Compassion helps to build strong bonds for lasting friendship. Studies have showed that when people set a goal to support one another compassionately, they experienced increased satisfaction and growth in their common endeavors.

- Compassion helps to mould us into characters that are less vindictive, less jealous and less selfish.

- Compassion helps us strengthen our moral principles and that contributes to build a cohesive team, group, or society.

- Compassion at work has been proven to boost productivity, lower employee turnover and maximize reward to all stakeholders.

- Studies have proven that societies that are more compassionate have less destitute, lower crime rates and generally, more happiness.

- Compassion makes people more socially adept, less vulnerable to loneliness, anger and depression. These in turn reduce stress that cause harm to the immune systems leading to healthier, longer and happier lives.

The following are some of the tips that can help you build and boost your compassion;

- See the good in others – Everyone has a positive side in life. Focusing overly on the negative negates our spirit of compassion.

- Focus on commonalities rather than differences – We are all different. This is the essence of diversity. However, focusing on what differentiates us than what which unites us will rob our sense compassion.

- Calm your inner worries - You cannot be compassionate if you are overwhelmed by inner worries, anxiety and regrets. The best way to calm your inner worries is through mindfulness and meditation.

- Encourage cooperation rather than competition – Competition draws the animal instinct in us that seeks to override or even trample on others in order to achieve success. This denies us the desire for compassion. When we cooperate see the importance of others in our joint endeavor and the desire to help them for all of us to succeed.

- See people as beings rather than objects – When you focus so much on the product rather than the people producing it, you end seeing people as objects of production rather than human beings who have senses, feelings and emotions. This makes you less compassionate.

- Avoid playing the blame game – Not all of us are fortunate. Some are less fortunate. Blaming people for their misfortunes rather than seeking to help them overcome them or relieve their harsh effects robs us of our compassion.

- Help to prevent inequality – Inequality is bred by some feeling a sense of entitlement to a higher status than the rest.

- Learn to appreciate and enjoy your moments of compassion – The best way to reinforce your compassion is to see the good you've done to others and appreciate the benefit they have received rather than how they have responded to you compassion. This way, you wouldn't regret when some become thankless.

- In acts of compassion, avoid absorbing the problem – It is easy to get so absorbed into acts of compassion such that we absorb the problem. Help others as much as you can but not more than you can as this can drain off your energy, lead to fatigue and more problems to your health thus cutting down on your compassion lifespan.

- Cultivate compassion in others – Teach your children, your family, your friends and your community about compassion. This is the best way to spread the goodness and also the best way to lower the burden that you shoulder in exercising compassion.

Practicing Self Compassion

Self-compassion is being considerate enough to understand your world flows from inside into the outer world. What gets out reflects that which is inside. Self-compassion is not selfishness or denying others of compassion but realizing that ultimately, like that vehicle that ferries others, it has to be well within its engine to make the journey safer, enjoyable and achievable. Thus, self-compassion is a kind of compassion turned inside out.

To practice self-compassion is to be in love with your being. It is to know without self-love actualized through action to relieve yourself of your very own challenges and suffering, you cannot achieve the same of others. You have to begin from inside. You have to tend to your own wound with tender love and understanding its sources and its eventual end. You have to heal your own wounds. Only then, can you be able to do the same of others. Having self-love accompanied by faith in your being is the true healing balm to your trauma when life hurts.

Love is the fuel that drives compassion. Without love, compassion cannot exist. To be compassionate is to express love in deeds. There is no way you can love others without first loving yourself. All else will be pretence. Love radiates from inside to outside. Without it being inside, it can't be outside.

When it comes to love and compassion, you can only receive as much as you give. Thus, if you have to love yourself dearly, then, you have to love others dearly for it is in loving others that you are capable of loving yourself and not the other way round. Thus, self-compassion must, for its very own survival, be externalized into compassion for others. This is where it derives its muscular strength and fitness.

Self-pity, anger, remorse, bitterness are all life hurts that are symptomatic of pain for that which happened in the past. They are signs of lack of happiness. It is not that you cannot be happy with pain. But, pain must not degenerate into self-pity, anger, remorse and bitterness. You must own your pain. To own it is to accept that what happened is irreversible and it had its own consequences which you are experiencing right now. You have to detach yourself from this sensitivity and experience pain for what it really is – a crying call for healing. Focus on healing.

Be nice to yourself

Life is tough sometimes. Acceptance of pain without reacting to it brings emotional intelligence. Treat yourself for 10 minutes a day with a soft word, a hand on your heart, and a level of understanding that what you are going through is painful. You are human, and as a human, you will experience pain and suffering. If you try to avoid this emotional experience through avoidance behaviours such as drugs or alcohol, you suffer further.

How to impact people's lives for many years after you are gone

Eternally impacting people is never such an easy adventure. It involves quite a lot. The following are steps involved in impacting on people's lives for many years long after you are gone:

1. **Explore people** – In exploring people, you make an active decision to get to know people. This conscious undertaking involves exploring people's culture, lifestyle, mindset, habits, attitudes and the like.

2. **Learn people** – In learning about people, you evaluate the outcome of your exploration; and do a further analysis of this outcome and draw out conclusions.

3. **Understand people** – To understand people is to comprehend the lessons drawn from learning about them.

4. **Accept people** – In accepting people, you accept people the way they are (based on your understanding of them) without apportioning judgment, opinions, biases and prejudices.

5. **Appreciate people** – To appreciate people is to accept them and know that in them there is a higher good in their humanness.

6. **Educate people** – Understanding, accepting and appreciating people is not about surrendering to their state of being. It is arriving to the greater good in them. Once you arrive at the greater good in them, you seek, through education, to advance this greater good so that greater benefit can be derived from them for the better of humanity. There is a Chinese proverb that goes: if you want to plan for a season, plant rice; if you want to plan for a decade, plant tree; if you plan for a lifetime, educate people.

7. **Uplift people** – Once you educate people, they become enlightened. They become to that self-awareness and awareness of the environment and their role in their being, the nature of beings and nature of things. To uplift them is to empower them with the necessary resources so that that they can attain a higher level of greater good.

8. **Inspire people** – Once people are uplifted, they need to be self-propelled in order to continue climbing the

staircase of greatness. They need to draw that inner energy inherent in them to achieve this. Lack of motivation or willpower can prevent them from achieving this. To inspire people is to ignite this willpower in them to draw upon this inherent energy into propelling themselves to higher pedestals of greater good.

SIX HABITS TO CULTIVATE

Mindfulness is achieved through habits. The following are key habits to cultivate in order to boost your mindfulness;

1. Learning habits
2. Social and communication habits
3. Spiritual habits
4. Personal care habits
5. Diet and fitness habits
6. Rest and relaxation habits

Learning habits

As Mahatma Gandhi once said "Live as if you were to die tomorrow and learn as if you were to live forever", learning is eternal. This is also emphasized by Buddha's teachings that learning is the greatest source of enlightenment and which is the only possible way by which you can overcome suffering. King Solomon of the old Bible is credited for having asked God for nothing but wisdom. Wisdom is intelligence gathered through learning experience.

Learning is the process of gathering knowledge. Learning can be accomplished through many ways including observing, watching, listening, reading, exploring, among others. Reading, listening and experiencing are some of the greatest ways to learn.

To enhance learning habits;

- Listen carefully before you respond
- Open yourself to new experiences.

Social and Communication habits

Humans are social beings. Without socializing, we struggle to live. However, the greatest victim of our modernity is socialization. Technology of convenience has substituted most of our physical interactions with electronic interactions. We find friends on Facebook and other social networks. We chat via Whatsapp, Skype, Hangouts, Twitter and such other chatting networks. We go to school via eLearning and telecommute to work. Avenues for social interactions are actively shrinking and so is the declining importance of social and communication habits in our academic and professional curriculum.

Yet, the number of people crying out for genuine and lasting relationships keeps on soaring. Friendships that used to be natural are becoming rare. Social ills such as suicide, terrorism and others are on the rise. This is simply because our social habits are on their deathbed. Although studies continue to assert that there are various forms of intelligence and there is increased recognition of social and emotional intelligence as the core competence of a well-formed human being, there is little effort to re-invigorating the importance of social habits.

In case you've not been taught about these social habits, we recap them here. These are just a few habits relating to everyday social and business engagements – greetings and communication.

To enhance social and communication habits;

- Always shake hands warmly with smile
- Be courteous when addressing people

Spiritual habits

Some argue that we are physical beings with a spiritual domain while others assert that we are spiritual beings with physical domain. Whatever the case, the role of spirituality in our beings cannot be overlooked. Though, there are many definitions and interpretations of what is meant by being spiritual or spirituality. We can simply look at a spirit as being that part of our invisible being that transcendent our physical realms. Spirituality is being above self and its limitations.

There are many habits that help to strengthen our spirituality thus helping us live happy and fulfilling lives. The following are just but a few of them;

- Speak your mind.
- Pray and/or meditate frequently
- Give yourself plenty of time
- Don't get worked up over things that won't matter tomorrow

Personal care habits

Cleanliness is next to Godliness. Cleanliness is not just the external cleanliness of the body. But it is also about the internal cleanliness of your body, mind and soul. Your outlook is the perfect mirror of your cleanliness. Always feel great about your outlook.

Diet and Fitness Habits

There is nothing holier than a good diet. Your body and wellbeing depends on your diet. Studies have found that over 70% of illnesses are either directly or indirectly related to diet. Diet is the source of your energy, source of your vitality and source of your longevity. Diet is what makes you live and alive now. It is not surprising that in the Biblical story of creation that the first man and woman were placed in the abundance of food, to gather and eat. Still in the Promised Land, milk and honey were the emblematic promise. If there is anything more holy than anything else, it is your diet. Do observe it as religiously as you would do anything and taking it spiritually and as holy as you can, for your health and wellbeing gravitates around it--- it is your world. Live no pretence!

Having a good diet is not just about eating food, it is making long-term, deliberate and sustained effort to nourish your body with its key essentials so that you live a healthy and happy life. Dietary Habits count! They are the invisible religious elements of your menu. Observe the following 9 habits of good dieting and you would have made it success.

- Drink Enough Water

- Take a Multivitamin

- Keep a food journal that includes not just what you ate but why and how you felt about it after

- Keep cut up fruits and Vegetables handy for snacks

- Cook a meal with one new ingredient every week.

- Make a list of unhealthy foods you don't love, then give yourself permission to not eat them.

- Limit alcoholic beverages to times when you really enjoy it.

- Cut out bad sugar.

- Cut out soda and artificial sweeteners.

- Walk 10,000 steps Daily.

- Stretch Every Day.

- Move Around Every Hour.

Rest and relaxation habits

Rest is one of the most important moments of your body. Unfortunately, it is one of those moments that are scarcely allocated time. Many people only count rest as sleep during bed-time when they are forced by nature or lack of night-work opportunities. Ideally, your body should rest at least 3/5 of your 24-hour day including 8 hours of quality undisrupted sleep. Planning for rest and enjoying a good sleep are the key elements of a good rest and relaxation habits.

- Plan for your rest and relaxation as you would plan for your other important activities.
- Get Enough Sleep.

With these 6 key habits, you are on your to ensuring long-term sustainable mindfulness.

CONCLUSION

Thank you for acquiring and reading this book.

This book introduces you to mindfulness. It further shows you can practice mindfulness to regain your focus and concentration, manage anger and hurt, deal with your stress and worry, and ultimately, promote compassion and peace. It also provides you with six powerful habits that you need to cultivate in order to successfully practice mindfulness in your everyday endeavors.

It is my sincere hope that you have been able to learn what mindfulness is, and, more importantly, embarked on practicing it. It is also my sincere hope that, you have been able to share with others this little book of knowledge of mindfulness so that, they too benefit from mindfulness.

Again, thank you for acquiring and reading this book.

Good luck.

www.ingramcontent.com/pod-product-compliance
Lightning Source LLC
Chambersburg PA
CBHW071247020426
42333CB00015B/1660